UXBRIDGE COLLEGE

Learning Resource Centre
Park Road, Uxbridge, Middlesex, UB81NQ
Renewals: 01895 853344

Please return this item to the LRC on or before the
last date stamped below:

D1486367

V&A PATTERN

SPITALFIELDS SILKS

First published by V&A Publishing, 2011
This revised edition published by V&A Publishing in 2020

Victoria and Albert Museum
South Kensington
London SW7 2RL
vam.ac.uk/publishing

Distributed in North America by Abrams, an imprint of ABRAMS

ISBN 978 1 83851 018 3

10 9 8 7 6 5 4 3 2 1
2024 2023 2022 2021 2020

A catalogue record for this book is available
from the British Library.

Cover images: see plates 3, 9, 22, 1, 17, 21, 27, 36

Pages 2–3: James Leman, design for a silk. Pencil, watercolour and
bodycolour on paper. UK, c.1721 (V&A: E.4450–1909)

Page 6: James Leman, design for a silk. Pencil, pen and ink, watercolour
and bodycolour on paper. UK, 1706–7 (V&A: E.1861:35–1991)

Page 11: Anna Maria Garthwaite, design for a silk. Pencil, watercolour
and bodycolour on paper. UK, 1733 (V&A: 5975:17)

Pages 78–9: Batchelor, Ham & Perigal, sample from a pattern book.
Woven silk. UK, 1782 (V&A: T.377:69–1972)

New series design: Jevon Hall

Colour Origination: DL Imaging, London
Printed in China

V&A Publishing
Supporting the world's leading
museum of art and design,
the Victoria and Albert
Museum, London

V&A Pattern

The Victoria and Albert Museum holds more than three million designs for textiles, decorations, wallpapers and prints. Each book in the *V&A Pattern* series offers a window into a part of this remarkably diverse collection.

The art of pattern-making, in all its forms and across the centuries, is revealed through the illustration of works by some of the greatest names in design history, shown alongside rarely seen treasures from pattern books, swatch books, company archives, design records and catalogues.

Featuring a concise expert introduction, the books are intended to be both beautiful and useful, presenting patterns to enjoy in their own right and as inspiration for new design.

Other titles in the *V&A Pattern* series include:

Indian Florals, introduced by Rosemary Crill
Kimono, introduced by Anna Jackson
William Morris, introduced by Linda Parry

Spitalfields Silks

Moira Thunder

In the eighteenth-century the area of Spitalfields, which was then just north of London's walls, was a major centre for European silk weaving. Weavers there produced silks that were among the most expensive and fashionable dress fabrics of the times, and this book includes a selection of the watercolour designs and woven silks they made from the early eighteenth century to the mid-1820s.

Located close to court – then the epicentre of fashion – Spitalfields weavers absorbed the latest styles as they were introduced by diplomats and other visitors from the continent. While the tailoring and cuts of dress changed slowly, the patterns woven into the silks changed seasonally and ultimately determined garments' fashionability. Portraits made between 1713 and 1750 show British and European royalty and nobility wearing rich silks, often brocaded in gold and silver threads, while the gentry and members of wealthy families are depicted in plainer styles. Mercers, or retailers, based in Ludgate Hill and Covent Garden commissioned silks from Spitalfields weavers, who in turn delegated some of the actual weaving to their journeymen. The mercers then sold the silks on to their rich and fashionable clientele, whose tailors or servants produced the desired garments.

Many silk weavers in England were French Huguenots who, having fled persecution in France, began to trade in Spitalfields; they include James Leman (*c.*1688–1745) and Christopher Baudouin (*c.*1665–1736), whose designs are shown here.

Indigenous talent is represented by English pattern drawers Joseph Dandridge (1660–1746) and Anna Maria Garthwaite (1690–1763). Spitalfields weavers, regardless of national background, all faced stiff competition from France, particularly from weavers based in Lyons. French innovations in weaving technology resulted in high-quality silks with wonderful designs that challenged the English industry's growth. By 1766, however, isolationist acts passed by government had banned textile imports to protect the silk industry from foreign competition. As a result, the Spitalfields silk industry flourished and even exported to the American colonies.

While Leman was both a designer and master weaver, most designers in the trade were independent pattern drawers who focused solely on creating patterns. Such work, however, still demanded a thorough understanding of the weaving process in order to produce patterns that were at once attractive *and* feasible. Different types of metal threads were identified by using strong reds and yellows as colour codes (plates 9 and 12). Another professional, who was not normally the pattern drawer in eighteenth-century England, but could be by the early 1800s, transferred the design onto ruled paper divided into squares corresponding to the warp and weft threads of a woven textile. The pattern was thus enlarged four to six times the scale of the original so that the individual threads became visible. The professional then applied bodycolour transparent enough to show the grid beneath the layer of colour. From the resulting ruled design, a 'reader' (*liseuse* in France) instructed a lash maker which lashes or loops of cord to tie around the relevant piece of the loom, enabling the weaver to produce the desired pattern. Different weaving techniques produced various types of textile, such as damask brocaded in coloured silks (plate 4) or satin ground brocaded with gold threads and details in coloured silks (plate 28).

In the mid-twentieth century, textile historians took to describing patterns produced between 1700 and 1710 as 'bizarre' because of their strange shapes and combinations of motifs (plates 4, 6 and 8). These styles evolved into what was later termed a 'luxuriant' phase, with patterns resembling jungle vegetation (plates 22 and 23), followed thereafter by patterns featuring ornamental surrounds that enclose symmetrical point repeats (plates 32 and 34). Between 1720 and 1732, designs with patterned areas similar to lace became popular (plate 42), but then fashions changed again when the introduction of skirts stretched over wide hoops led to a demand for larger motifs.

By 1742, heavy forms were replaced by a new naturalism that broke from such styles. These distinctly English patterns featured floral sprigs – often identifiable flowers such as carnations and auricula (plates 49, 50, 51 and 52) – scattered lightly over a pale ground. They reflected the English love of gardens and remained popular throughout the 1740s and early 1750s. In the mid-1750s, patterns still featured light arrangements but with motifs woven in metal threads acting as foils to flowers (plates 57 and 58). Smaller patterns featuring sprigs and natural forms, including scallop shells, came into favour, such as those probably produced by the firm Batchelor, Ham & Perigal (plates 60 and 61). Spitalfields silks continue to have enduring appeal today and those original textile firms that survive often turn to their company archives to locate centuries-old designs and textiles that still astonish observers with their éclat.

1
James Leman, design for a silk
Pencil, pen and ink, watercolour and bodycolour on paper. UK, 1706–7 (V&A: E.1861:15–1991)

2
James Leman, design for a silk
Pencil, pen and ink, watercolour and bodycolour on paper. UK, 1707 (V&A: E.1861:6–1991)

3
James Leman, design for a silk
Pencil, pen and ink, watercolour and bodycolour on paper. UK, 1707 (V&A: E.1861:46–1991)

4
Dress fabric
Woven silk damask brocaded with coloured silks. UK, c.1707–8 (V&A: 711–1864)

5
James Leman, design for a silk
Pencil, pen and ink, and watercolour on paper. UK, 1710 (V&A: E.1861:84–1991)

6
James Leman, design for a silk
Pencil, pen and ink, and watercolour on paper. UK, 1710 (V&A: E.1861:72–1991)

7
James Leman, design for a silk
Pencil, pen and ink, and watercolour on paper. UK, 1709 (V&A: E.1861:95–1991)

8
Dress fabric
Woven satin with patterning wefts of silver thread. UK, c.1708 (V&A: T.3–1994)

9
James Leman, design for a silk
Pencil, pen and ink, and watercolour on paper. UK, 1717 (V&A: E.4440–1909)

10
James Leman, design for a silk
Pencil, pen and ink, and bodycolour on paper. UK, 1720 (V&A: E.4456–1909)

11
James Leman, design for a silk
Pencil, pen and ink, watercolour and bodycolour on paper. UK, c.1719 (V&A: E.4517–1909)

12
Joseph Dandridge, design for a silk
Pencil and watercolour on paper. UK, 1718 (V&A: E.4466–1909)

13
James Leman, design for a silk
Pencil, pen and ink, watercolour and bodycolour on paper. UK, 1720 (V&A: E.4459–1909)

14
Joseph Dandridge, design for a silk
Pencil, pen and ink, and watercolour on paper. UK, 1720 (V&A: E.4514–1909)

15
Joseph Dandridge, design for a silk
Pencil, pen and ink, and watercolour on paper. UK, 1720 (V&A: E.4453–1909)

16
James Leman, design for a silk
Pencil, pen and ink, and watercolour on paper. UK, 1721 (V&A: E.4455–1909)

17
Probably James Leman, design for a silk
Pencil, watercolour and bodycolour on paper. UK, 1719 (V&A: E.4443–1909)

18
Joseph Dandridge, design for a silk
Pencil, pen and ink, and watercolour on paper. UK, 1720 (V&A: E.4518–1909)

19
James Leman, design for a silk
Pencil, pen and ink, watercolour and bodycolour on paper. UK, 1718 (V&A: E.4468–1909)

20
James Leman, design for a silk
Pencil, pen and ink, watercolour and bodycolour on paper. UK, 1720 (V&A: E.4503–1909)

21
James Leman, design for a silk
Pencil, watercolour and bodycolour on paper. UK, 1719 (V&A: E.4472–1909)

22
James Leman, design for a silk
Pencil, pen and ink, watercolour and bodycolour on paper. UK, 1719 (V&A: E.4511–1909)

23
James Leman, design for a silk
Pencil, pen and ink, and watercolour on paper. UK, 1721 (V&A: E.4446–1909)

24
James Leman, design for a silk
Pencil, pen and ink, watercolour and bodycolour on paper. UK, 1720 (V&A: E.4484–1909)

25
Joseph Dandridge, design for a silk
Pencil, watercolour and bodycolour on paper. UK, 1720 (V&A: E.4441–1909)

26
Joseph Dandridge, design for a silk
Pencil, pen and ink, watercolour and bodycolour on paper. UK, 1721 (V&A: E.4505–1909)

27
Possibly James Leman, design for a silk
Pencil, watercolour and bodycolour on paper. UK, 1726–9 (V&A: 5973:16)

28
Segment from George II's Coronation Canopy
Woven satin brocaded with gold thread and coloured silks. UK, 1726–7 (V&A: T.184–1975)

29
Christopher Baudouin, design for a silk
Pencil and watercolour on paper. UK, 1723–4 (V&A: 5973:17)

30
Robe
Woven satin patterned in coloured silks. UK, 1725–30 (V&A: T.180–1962)

31
Anna Maria Garthwaite, design for a silk
Pencil, watercolour and bodycolour on paper. UK, *c.*1732 (V&A: 5975:8)

32
Christening mantle
Woven silk brocaded with coloured silks. UK, c.1728 (V&A: T.76–1936)

33
Christopher Baudouin, design for a silk
Pencil, pen and ink, and watercolour on paper. UK, c.1726 (V&A: 5973:6)

34
Dress fabric
Woven silk brocaded with coloured silks. UK, 1724–5 (V&A: T.18–1969)

35
Anna Maria Garthwaite, design for a silk
Pencil and watercolour on paper. UK, 1726–7 (V&A: 5970:3)

36
Anna Maria Garthwaite, design for a silk
Pencil and watercolour on paper. UK, 1726–7 (V&A: 5970:16)

37
Anna Maria Garthwaite, design for a silk
Pencil and watercolour on paper. UK, c.1726 (V&A: 5970:11)

38
Anna Maria Garthwaite, design for a silk
Pencil and watercolour on paper. UK, 1726–8 (V&A: 5970:21)

39
Anna Maria Garthwaite, design for a silk
Pencil, pen and ink, and watercolour on paper. UK, c.1726 (V&A: 5970:1)

40
Anna Maria Garthwaite, design for a silk
Pencil, pen and ink, and watercolour on paper. UK, 1727 (V&A: 5970:46)

41
Anna Maria Garthwaite, design for a silk
Pencil and watercolour on paper. UK, 1733 (V&A: 5975:9)

42
Anna Maria Garthwaite, design for a silk
Pencil and watercolour on paper. UK, c.1730 (V&A: 5975:2)

43
Dress fabric
Woven silk brocaded with coloured silks. UK, c.1734 (V&A: T.26–1966)

44
Dress fabric
Woven silk brocaded with coloured silks. UK, *c*.1734 (V&A: T.99–1912)

45
Anna Maria Garthwaite, design for a silk
Pencil, watercolour and bodycolour on paper. UK, 1738 (V&A: 5977:11)

46
Dress fabric
Woven silk brocaded with coloured silks. UK, *c.*1740 (V&A: T.347–1910)

47
Anna Maria Garthwaite, design for a silk
Pencil, watercolour and bodycolour on paper. UK, 1741 (V&A: 5979:6)

48
Anna Maria Garthwaite, design for a silk
Pencil, pen and ink, watercolour and bodycolour on paper. UK, 1742 (V&A: 5980:13)

49
Anna Maria Garthwaite, design for a silk (see also plate 50)
Pencil, pen and ink, watercolour and bodycolour on paper. UK, 1747 (V&A: 5985:2)

50
Possibly Daniel Vautier, gown (see also plate 49)
Woven silk tobine brocaded with coloured silks. UK, 1747 (V&A: T.706–1913)

51
Anna Maria Garthwaite, design for a silk (see also plate 52)
Pencil, pen and ink, and watercolour on paper. UK, 1744 (V&A: 5982:10)

52
Gown (see also plate 51)
Woven satin brocaded with coloured silks. UK, 1744 (V&A: T.264–1966)

53
Anna Maria Garthwaite, design for a silk (see also plate 54)
Pencil, pen and ink, and watercolour on paper. UK, 1747 (V&A: 5985:9)

54
Possibly Daniel Vautier, dress (see also plate 53)
Woven silk lustring brocaded with coloured silks. UK, 1747 (V&A: T.720–1913)

55
Anna Maria Garthwaite, design for a silk (see also plate 56)
Pencil, pen and ink, and watercolour on paper. UK, 1749 (V&A: 5987:1)

56
Possibly Daniel Vautier (see also plate 55)
Woven silk tobine brocaded with coloured silks. UK, 1749 (V&A: T.192–1996)

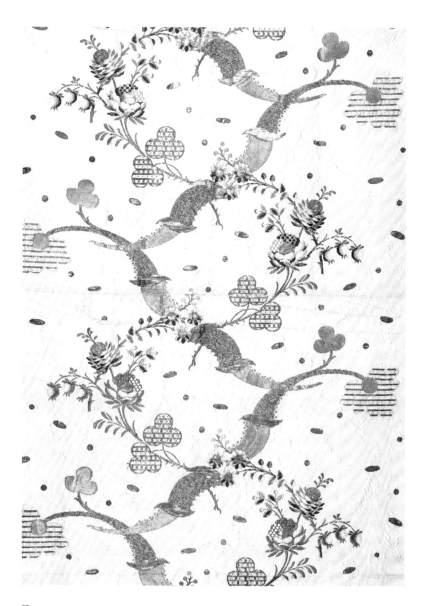

57
Dress fabric
Woven silk brocaded with silver-gilt thread and coloured silks. UK, 1750–55 (V&A: Circ.513–1931)

58
Dress fabric
Woven silk brocaded with silver thread and coloured silks. UK, 1750–60 (V&A: T.161A–1959)

59
Dress fabric
Woven silk brocaded with coloured silks. UK, 1744–7 (V&A: T.147–1973)

60
Probably Batchelor, Ham & Perigal, sample from a pattern book
Woven silk tobine. UK, c.1755–65 (V&A: T.375:17–1972)

61
Probably Batchelor, Ham & Perigal, samples from a pattern book
Woven silk in different colourways. UK, 1763–5 (V&A: T.375:311–1972)

62
Batchelor, Ham & Perigal, samples from a pattern book
Woven silk in different colourways. UK, 1768–80 (V&A: T.374:1–1972)

63
Jourdain and John Ham, sample from a pattern book
Woven silk in different colourways. UK, 1816–26 (V&A: T.385:154–1972)

64
Jourdain and John Ham, samples from a pattern book
Woven silk in different colourways. UK, 1816–26 (V&A: T.385:189–1972)

65
Sample from a pattern book
Woven silk in different colourways. UK, 1816–26 (V&A: T.385:121–1972)

66
Jourdain and John Ham, sample from a pattern book
Woven silk in different colourways. UK, 1816–26 (V&A: T.385:250–1972)

Further Reading

Browne, Clare
'The Influence of Botanical
Sources on Early 18th-Century
English Silk Design'
in *Eighteenth-Century Silks:
The Industries of England
and Northern Europe*
Riggisberg, 2000 (pp.25–38)

Cabrera-Lafuente, Ana and
Miller, Lesley Ellis, eds
with Allen-Johnstone, Claire
Silk: Fibre, Fabric and Fashion
London, 2021

Miller, Lesley Ellis
'Between Engraving and
Silk Manufacture in Late
Eighteenth-Century Lyons:
Marie-Anne Bernier and
Other Point Papermakers'
in *Studies in the Decorative
Arts* Vol.3, 1995–6 (pp. 52–76)

Miller, Lesly Ellis
*Selling Silks: A Merchant's
Sample Book 1764*
London, 2014

Parry, Linda, intro.
*British Textiles: 1700
to the Present*
London, 2010

Rothstein, Natalie
*Silk Designs of the
Eighteenth Century in the
Collection of the Victoria
and Albert Museum*
London, 1990

Thornton, Peter
Baroque and Rococo Silks
London, 1965